Enrich Book

Grade 3

PROVIDES Daily Enrichment Activities

 HOUGHTON MIFFLIN HARCOURT

Table of Contents

Chapter 3: Understand Multiplication

Chapter 4: Multiplication Facts and Strategies

Chapter 5: Use Multiplication Facts

Chapter 6: Understand Division

Chapter 7: Division Facts and Strategies

CRITICAL AREA: Fractions

Chapter 8: Understand Fractions

Chapter 9: Compare Fractions

CRITICAL AREA: Measurement

Chapter 10: Time, Length, Liquid Volume, and Mass

Chapter 11: Perimeter and Area

CRITICAL AREA: Geometry
Chapter 12: Two-Dimensional Shapes

Pattern Pairs and Quads

+	0	1	2	3	4	5	6	7	8	9
0	0	1	2	3	4	5	6	7	8	9
1	1	2	3	4	5	6	7	8	9	10
2	2	3	4	5	6	7	8	9	10	11
3	3	4	5	6	7	8	9	10	11	12
4	4	5	6	7	8	9	10	11	12	13
5	5	6	7	8	9	10	11	12	13	14
6	6	7	8	9	10	11	12	13	14	15
7	7	8	9	10	11	12	13	14	15	16
8	8	9	10	11	12	13	14	15	16	17
9	9	10	11	12	13	14	15	16	17	18

1. Look at a pair of numbers next to each other in any *row* of the addition table. Is their sum even or odd? **Explain.**

_____

_____

2. Look at a pair of numbers next to each other in any *column* of the addition table. Is their sum even or odd? **Explain.**

_____

_____

3. Stretch Your Thinking Look at any square of four numbers in the addition table. One square is outlined as an example. Is the sum of the four numbers even or odd? **Explain.**

_____

_____

_____

Round and About

Round the distances to the nearest hundred and ten.

		Nearest Hundred	Nearest Ten
1.	628 miles	_____ miles	_____ miles
2.	704 miles	_____ miles	_____ miles
3.	58 miles	_____ miles	_____ miles

4. **Write Math** ➤ **Explain** why 58 can be rounded to the nearest hundred even though there is not a digit in the hundreds place.

_____

_____

_____

5. **Stretch Your Thinking** Write a number that is the same when rounded to the nearest hundred and ten. **Explain.**

_____

_____

_____

_____

Estimating the Crowd

It is Kids' Month at the city baseball park. The table shows
how many people went to the baseball games during Kids'
Month. Estimate to answer each question.

Attendance		
Game	Adults	Children
Game 1	235	324
Game 2	257	399
Game 3	189	404
Game 4	477	398
Game 5	317	197

1. Which game did the fewest people attend? _____

2. Which game did about 650 people attend? _____

3. Which game did the most people attend? _____

4. **Stretch Your Thinking** Suppose the total attendance at Game 6
   was about 800 and there were more children than adults at
   the game. About how many children and how many adults could
   have attended? **Explain** how you know your answer is correct.

   _____

   _____

   _____

   _____

Name _____

Musical Math

Use mental math strategies to solve the problem.

Use this information for 1–3.

There are 35 more musicians in the String section of a city Symphony Orchestra than in its Brass section. There are 29 musicians in the Brass section.

1. How many musicians in all are in the String and Brass sections of the Symphony Orchestra?

   _____

2. Suppose 2 more musicians joined the String section of the Symphony Orchestra, and 4 musicians left the Brass section. How many musicians in all would there be in the String and Brass sections?

   _____

3. How many musicians would the city Symphony Orchestra need to add now to have at least 100 musicians in its String and Brass sections?

   _____

Use this information for 4–6.

The String section of a city Symphony Orchestra has 10 more musicians playing First and Second Violins than Violas and Cellos. It has 23 Violas and Cellos.

4. How many First and Second Violins, Violas, and Cellos are in the Symphony Orchestra?

   _____

5. Suppose the Symphony Orchestra added 2 Violas and 2 Cellos. How many musicians would be in the String section of the Symphony Orchestra then?

   _____

6. How many String musicians would the Symphony Orchestra need to add now to have exactly 75 musicians in its String section?

   _____

7. **Write Math** ▸ How do mental math strategies help you solve problems such as the ones above?

_____

_____

Properties on Parade

**Use addition properties to find the unknown numbers.
Write the property that you used.**

1. $(\blacksquare + 7) + 30 = 47$

_____

_____

2. $(44 + 8) + 52 = \blacksquare + (\blacksquare + 52)$

_____

_____

3. $(96 + 7) + 73 = \blacksquare + (\blacksquare + 73)$

_____

_____

4. $(9 + 17) + \blacksquare = 59$

_____

_____

5. $(\blacksquare + 3) + 75 = 98$

_____

_____

6. $5 + \blacksquare + 65 = 89$

_____

_____

7. **Write Math** ▶ **Explain** how using addition properties can make adding easier.

_____

_____

_____

Name _____

Find the Errors

**Find the error in each problem. Describe the error.
Then write the correct sum.**

1. Asha used the break apart strategy to find 405 + 503. She added the place values and got 980.

$$400 + 50 + 0$$
$$+ 500 + 30 + 0$$
$$900 + 80 + 0 = 980$$

_____

_____

2. Mick used the break apart strategy to find 580 + 348. He added the place values and got 828.

$$500 + 80 + 0$$
$$+ 300 + 40 + 8$$
$$800 + 120 + 8 = 828$$

_____

_____

3. Karl used the break apart strategy to find 409 + 325 and got a sum of 814.

$$400 + 90 + 9$$
$$+ 300 + 20 + 5$$
$$700 + 110 + 4 = 814$$

_____

_____

4. **Write Math** ▶ Why is it important to write any zero in the correct place-value position when using the break apart strategy to add?

_____

_____

_____

Back and Forth Addition

A *palindrome* reads the same forward as it does backward.

Forward		Backward
mom	$\longrightarrow$	mom
deed	$\longrightarrow$	deed

A number can also be a palindrome.

Forward		Backward
22	$\longrightarrow$	22
313	$\longrightarrow$	313

Try This

Start with a 3-digit number: 142

Reverse it: 241

Add the two numbers: $142 + 241 = 383$

You get a palindrome!

You may need to reverse and add more than one time.

Find a palindrome. Show your work.

1. 125

_____

2. 207

_____

3. 316

_____

4. 443

_____

5. Write Math ► Sandy says that if you add two numbers that are palindromes, the sum will always be a palindrome. Do you agree? **Explain.**

_____

_____

6. Stretch Your Thinking Find a 3-digit number you can use to make a palindrome. Write your number. Then use it to make a palindrome.

_____

Estimating Pocket Change

**Charlie has a pair of pants with six different pockets labeled
A to F. Each pocket has a card for a number of coins inside.
The list below shows the number hidden in each pocket.**

Pocket

A = 394

B = 147

C = 610

D = 198

E = 782

F = 336

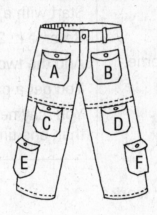

Estimate the difference.

1. Pocket E − Pocket B = _____

2. Pocket C − Pocket F = _____

3. Pocket A − Pocket B = _____

4. Pocket A − Pocket F = _____

5. Pocket D − Pocket B = _____

6. Pocket E − Pocket D = _____

7. **Write Math** ▸ For Exercise 5, Tom estimates 100 coins and Nina estimates 50 coins. Whose estimate is closer to the exact answer? **Explain**.

_____

_____

_____

_____

8. **Stretch Your Thinking**
Charlie has two back pockets with numbers for coins in each pocket. The difference between the numbers is about 150. What numbers could he have in each pocket? **Explain**.

_____

_____

_____

_____

Friendly Numbers Puzzle

Combine pairs of numerals in the puzzle pieces to form a
friendly subtraction to help you complete the table below.
Use each puzzle piece only once.

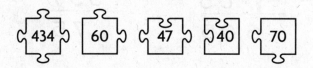

	Subtraction	Puzzle Piece 1		Puzzle Piece 2	Difference
1.	43 − 19		−		
2.	72 − 39		−		
3.	64 − 28		−		
4.	46 − 9		−		
5.	433 − 99		−		

6. **Write Math** ▸ Describe the strategy you used to find
the puzzle pieces to help you subtract in Exercise 3.

_____

_____

_____

_____

_____

Mystery Subtraction

Find the unknown digit.

1.
```
  426
- 1▮8
─────
  268
```

2.
```
  698
- 38▮
─────
  309
```

3.
```
  710
- ▮05
─────
  605
```

4.
```
  572
- 397
─────
 ▮75
```

5.
```
  543
- 29▮
─────
  249
```

6.
```
  475
- 2▮9
─────
  236
```

7.
```
  832
- 2▮8
─────
  554
```

8.
```
  986
- 67▮
─────
  308
```

9. **Write Math** ▶ **Explain** how you found the unknown digit in Exercise 6.

_____

_____

_____

10. **Stretch Your Thinking** What is the greatest 3-digit number you can subtract from 426 so that you would need to regroup? **Explain.**

_____

_____

_____

Recycling Problems

Solve the problem. Estimate first. Then write and solve a similar problem using different numbers.

1. Tim and Alex collected aluminum cans for recycling. Tim collected a total of 942 cans. Alex collected 327 cans. How many fewer cans did Alex collect than Tim?

   Estimate: _____

   Answer: _____ cans

   _____
   _____
   _____
   _____
   _____
   _____
   _____

2. Stewart collected 842 used tires to recycle. Angel collected 529 used tires. How many fewer tires did Angel collect than Stewart?

   Estimate: _____

   Answer: _____ tires

   _____
   _____
   _____
   _____
   _____
   _____
   _____

3. Yesterday, a recycling center collected 679 cans. The center collected 225 fewer bottles than cans, and 178 fewer newspaper bundles than bottles. How many newspaper bundles did the center collect yesterday?

   _____
   _____
   _____
   _____
   _____

   _____
   _____
   _____
   _____
   _____

Get the Picture?

The students at Audubon School voted for their favorite color. The color green had 164 votes. The color blue had 293 votes. The color red had 129 votes.

Draw a line to match the problem with the bar model that can be used to solve it. Then solve.

Problem	Bar Model

1. How many more students voted for blue than green?

   _____

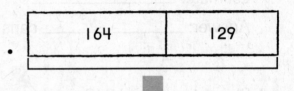

2. How many more students need to vote for red for it to have the same number of votes as blue?

   _____

3. **What if** 129 more students voted for green? How many votes would green have now?

   _____

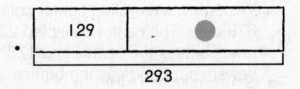

4. **What if** 129 more students voted for blue? How many votes would blue have now?

   _____

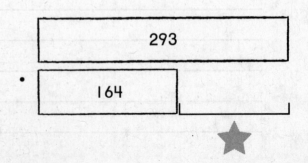

Find the Frequency

Mr. MacTavish's class started to make tally tables and frequency tables. The students did not finish the tables before the end of the day. Use the clues and data given to complete each table.

1. **Clue:** A total of 21 students voted for their favorite yogurt topping.

Favorite Yogurt Topping	
Type	Tally
Sprinkles	
Nuts	ⅣⅠⅠ
Fruit	

Favorite Yogurt Topping	
Type	
Sprinkles	
Nuts	
Fruit	6

2. **Clue:** The number of votes for summer is equal to 1 more than the sum of the votes for spring and fall together.

Favorite Season	
Season	Tally
Spring	ⅣⅠⅠ
Summer	
Fall	ⅣⅠⅠ
Winter	ⅣⅠⅠ ⅠⅠⅠ

Favorite Season	
	Number
	5
Summer	
Fall	5

3. **Stretch Your Thinking** What other clues could be used to find the missing data in Exercise 1? Write a different clue for the exercise.

_____

_____

_____

Name _____

Using Picture Keys

The key shows how many each picture stands for.

KEY
♥ = 3   ◆ = 5   ■ = 7   ▼ = 8

Use the key to complete the addition sentence.

1.

   3 + 3 + 8 + _____ + _____ + _____ + _____ = _____

2.

   _____ + _____ + _____ + _____ + _____ = _____

3.

   _____ + _____ + _____ + _____ + _____ = _____

4.

   _____ + _____ + _____ + _____ + _____ = _____

5. **Stretch Your Thinking** Draw four different combinations of pictures that represent a sum of 20.

Picture Perfect Pizza

Harrison surveyed 26 students about their favorite pizza topping. Complete the table at the right.

Favorite Pizza Topping	
Pizza Topping	Number of Students
Pepperoni	
Sausage	5
Mushrooms	6
Olives	7

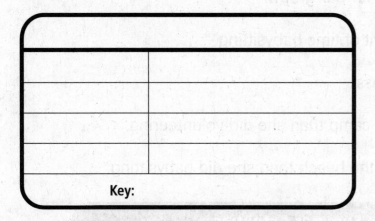

Key:

1. Use the data in the table to make a picture graph.

2. Which topping did most students choose?

_____

3. How many more students chose olives than chose sausage as their favorite topping?

4. How many fewer students chose pepperoni than chose sausage and mushrooms combined?

_____

5. **Write Math** ➤ Suppose two students were absent the day the survey was taken. When they returned to school, both students chose mushrooms as their favorite topping. How would the graph change?

_____

_____

_____

Summer Bar Graph

**Annabelle tells about her summer by using a bar graph.
She shows the number of days she spent doing each
activity, but forgets to write the activities! Use the clues
below to help Annabelle complete her bar graph.**

1. Annabelle spent the least amount of time babysitting.

2. Annabelle did not take an art class.

3. Annabelle spent 4 fewer days at camp than she did volunteering.

4. Annabelle spent 2 more days at the beach than she did babysitting.

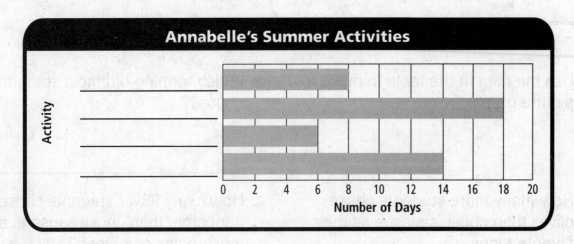

5. **Write Math** ➤ Which clue was the least helpful? **Explain**.

_____

_____

_____

6. **Stretch Your Thinking** Do you think the graph tells what
Annabelle did every day in the summer? **Explain**.

_____

_____

_____

Field Trip Survey

Ms. Klein surveyed some students to find where they wanted to go for a field trip. She gave them four choices and recorded the results in a table.

1. Make a bar graph to show the results of the survey.

Field Trip Choices	
Location	Number of Students
Art Museum	15
Science Center	21
Computer Museum	12
Zoo	24

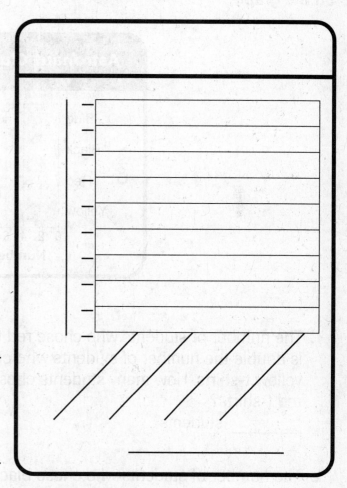

2. How many students in all were surveyed?

_____

3. Which location was chosen twice as often as computer museum?

_____

4. Which location was chosen more than the computer museum but less than the science center?

_____

5. Write Math ⮞ How would the graph change if 6 more students answered the survey and all chose the art museum?

_____

_____

_____

Name _____

Bar Graph Problems

**Sydney needs to complete the bar graph, but she
lost her frequency table with the data.
Use the clues about the data to draw each bar
on the graph.**

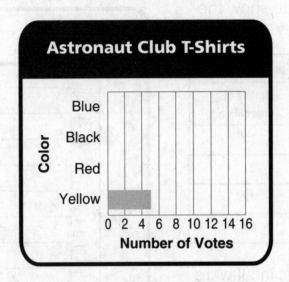

1. The number of students who chose red t-shirts
   is double the number of students who chose
   yellow t-shirts. How many students chose
   red t-shirts?

   _____ students

2. The number of students who chose black t-shirts
   is equal to the number of students who chose red
   and yellow t-shirts combined. How many students
   chose black t-shirts?

   _____ students

3. There were 7 fewer students who chose blue t-shirts
   than chose black t-shirts. How many students chose
   blue t-shirts?

   _____ students

The Plot Thickens!

Use the line plot below for 1–2.

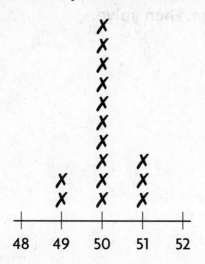

1. Jack forgot to write the title for this line plot. **Explain** why the line plot probably does not show ages of third graders.

_____

_____

_____

2. Write a title that makes sense for the line plot. **Explain** why you think it makes sense.

_____

_____

_____

Use the line plot below for 3–5.

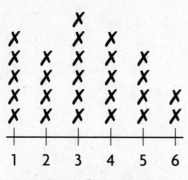

Number of Books Read over Summer Break

3. How many students read 5 or more books?

_____

4. How many students read the greatest number of books?

_____

5. **Write Math** ▸ Tell how you can use the data in the line plot to find the number of students who read over summer break.

_____

_____

Clues and Equal Groups

Read each problem. Look for a clue that tells about the number of groups. Draw equal groups to model the problem. Then solve.

1. Jan walks 4 miles each week for one month. How many miles does she walk altogether?

   _____

2. Brett signed up for 2 tennis lessons each month from January through May. How many lessons did he sign up for in all?

   _____

3. Miriam practices playing the clarinet for 2 hours every day. How many hours does she practice the clarinet each week?

   _____

4. **Write Math** ▶ Choose one of the problems. **Explain** how your drawing shows equal groups.

   _____

   _____

Name _____

Model Groups

Draw a quick picture to show equal groups. Then write related addition and multiplication sentences.

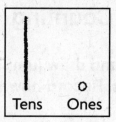

Tens Ones

1. 3 groups of 4

2. 2 groups of 11

_____

_____

3. 4 groups of 15

4. 3 groups of 12

_____

_____

5. **Write Math** ▸ Dalton is baking pepperoni pizza. He uses
11 pepperonis for every pizza. How many pizzas did he make
if he used 55 pepperonis? **Explain.**

_____

_____

Name _____

Skip Counting

Label and draw jumps on the number line to count equal groups. Record how to skip count to solve.

1. How many fingers are there on 4 hands?

   _____

   There are _____ fingers on 4 hands.

   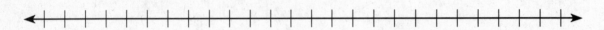

2. How many legs are there on 3 horses?

   _____

   There are _____ legs on 3 horses.

   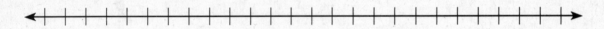

3. How many wheels are there on 6 cars?

   _____

   There are _____ wheels on 6 cars.

   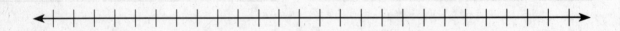

4. **Stretch Your Thinking** Write your own problem like the ones on this page. Trade with a classmate. Then solve.

   _____

   _____

Solve Problems with Bar Models

Use this information for 1–3.

On Monday, 4 students from Ms. Lee's class each checked out 3 books from the library. Then 2 students from Ms. Reeves' class each checked out 5 books.

1. Draw a bar model to show the number of books checked out by each student in each class.

2. On Monday, how many books were checked out of the library by these students?

   _____

3. On Tuesday, 3 other students from Ms. Lee's class went to the library and checked out 3 books each. How many students in all from Ms. Lee's class checked out books on Monday and Tuesday?

   _____

Use this information for 4–6.

Jason planted 8 tomato plants. Then he planted 3 groups of 8 squash plants.

4. Draw a bar model to show how many tomato plants and squash plants Jason planted.

5. How many tomato and squash plants did Jason plant in all?

   _____

6. How many more squash plants than tomato plants did Jason plant?

   _____

7. **Write Math** Use the given information for 1–3 to write a problem. Then solve your problem.

_____

_____

_____

Name _____

Garden Arrays

Ed's Garden Nursery is displaying new flowers. Each type of flower is arranged in an array. Use the clues to label each part of the flower display. Then find the number of each type of flower. Color the display.

1. Yellow mums 2×8 array = _____ mums

2. Purple pansies 6×4 array = _____ pansies

3. Pink begonias 5×5 array = _____ begonias

4. Orange marigolds 3×7 array = _____ marigolds

5. White petunias 3×4 array = _____ petunias

6. Blue tulips 3×8 array = _____ tulips

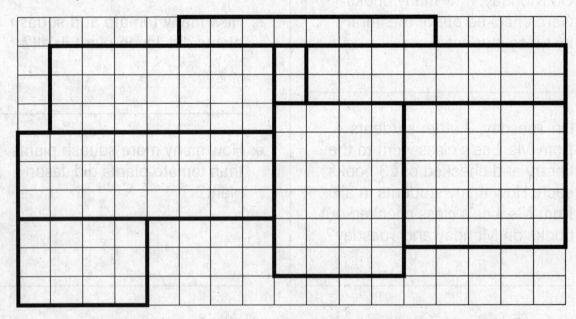

7. Add a 2×5 array for a red rose garden. Label it and color it red.

8. **Write Math** ▸ **Explain** how you decided where each type of flower belonged.

_____

Multiplication by Arrangement

Solve.

1. Sara made an array with 10 tiles. The array had 2 rows. How many tiles were in each row?

_____

2. Kelly put 15 jars of spices in the cabinet. There were 5 jars in each row. How many rows did Kelly make?

_____

3. Leslie wants to display 12 seashells in equal rows. She starts to draw this array.

What are two ways Leslie can complete the array?

_____

_____

_____

4. This array shows how José displays the 18 rocks in his collection.

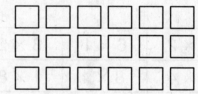

What are three other ways José can display his rocks in equal rows.

_____

_____

_____

5. Write Math ► Mark arranges cans in 8 rows with 3 cans in each row. Using the same total number of cans, how many different ways can Mark make equal rows of cans? List the ways.

_____

_____

Three in a Row

Find three facts in a row, column, or diagonally that have the same product. Circle the facts and write the product.

1.

6 × 1	1 × 3	3 × 0
1 × 0	2 × 3	0 × 2
2 × 6	2 × 1	1 × 6

Product = _____

2.

5 × 4	1 × 5	4 × 5
1 × 20	5 × 0	4 × 2
4 × 5	2 × 5	1 × 0

Product = _____

3.

4 × 2	6 × 1	3 × 2
2 × 4	8 × 1	1 × 8
2 × 6	4 × 6	0 × 6

Product = _____

4.

10 × 2	4 × 9	10 × 0
4 × 10	5 × 10	9 × 0
4 × 0	2 × 10	0 × 5

Product = _____

5.

1 × 10	5 × 10	5 × 2
10 × 0	2 × 5	1 × 5
10 × 1	2 × 10	2 × 1

Product = _____

6.

0 × 16	8 × 1	2 × 4
4 × 8	1 × 8	8 × 4
1 × 16	4 × 4	8 × 2

Product = _____

7. Stretch Your Thinking How are adding 0 and multiplying by 1 alike?

_____

_____

_____

What's My Number?

Solve each riddle.

1. I am a factor of 12. The other factor is 3. What number am I?

   _____

2. I am a factor of 12. The other factor is 2. What number am I?

   _____

3. I am a product. One of my factors is 2. The other factor is 1 greater than 4. What number am I?

   _____

4. I am a product. One of my factors is 7. The sum of my factors equals 11. What number am I?

   _____

5. I am a factor of 28. The other factor is 4. What number am I?

   _____

6. I am a factor of 32. The other factor is 4. What number am I?

   _____

7. I am a product. Both of my factors are the same number. The sum of my factors is 4. What number am I?

   _____

8. I am a product. One of my factors is 3. The other factor is 2 times as great. What number am I?

   _____

9. I am a factor of 18. The other factor is 9. What number am I?

   _____

10. I am a product. One of my factors is 9. The sum of my two factors is 13. What number am I?

    _____

11. I am a number that is four times the product of 2 and 3. One of my factors is 4. What is my other factor?

    _____

12. I am a number that is double the product of 2 and 7. One of my factors is 7. What is my other factor?

    _____

Unknown Numbers

Use the numbers in each oval to complete four different number sentences. Use each number in the oval only once.

1. $5 \times \square = \square$

$\square \times \square = 30$

$5 \times \square = \square$

$\square \times \square = 35$

Oval: 6 5 7 5
1 5 8 40

2. $\square \times \square = 70$

$10 \times \square = \square$

$10 \times \square = \square$

$\square \times \square = 40$

Oval: 4 10 10 2
7 20 90 9

3. $5 \times \square = \square$

$5 \times \square = \square$

$\square \times \square = 45$

$\square \times \square = 15$

Oval: 3 5 0 5
0 9 5 25

4. $\square \times \square = 20$

$10 \times \square = \square$

$\square \times \square = 10$

$10 \times \square = \square$

Oval: 7 10 10 2
6 60 70 1

5. **Write Math** ▶ How are all of the products in Exercise 4 alike?

_____

_____

Name _____

Products in Parentheses

For each exercise, multiply the numbers inside the parentheses first. Then add or subtract.

Find the answer in the code box. Write the code letter on the line above the exercise number at the bottom of the page to answer the riddle.

CODE

A	B	C	E	F	I	L	M	N	O	R	S	T	U	W	Y
7	8	9	10	11	13	14	15	16	20	21	28	29	31	33	35

1. $(5 \times 2) + (1 \times 3) =$ _____

2. $(6 \times 4) + (5 \times 1) =$ _____

3. $(7 \times 3) - (2 \times 5) =$ _____

4. $(3 \times 6) - (4 \times 2) =$ _____

5. $(2 \times 3) + (4 \times 2) =$ _____

6. $(9 \times 6) - (5 \times 5) =$ _____

7. $(9 \times 3) - (6 \times 3) =$ _____

8. $(1 \times 3) + (3 \times 6) =$ _____

9. $(3 \times 5) + (8 \times 2) =$ _____

10. $(3 \times 9) - (6 \times 2) =$ _____

11. $(3 \times 8) - (4 \times 4) =$ _____

12. $(4 \times 2) + (9 \times 3) =$ _____

Why did the cookie go to the doctor?

__ __   __ __ __ __   __ __ __ __ __ __
1 2   3 4 5 6   7 8 9 10 11 12

United Arrays

Draw an array for each clue. Then use the arrays to solve each problem.

1. Craig spent $27 to buy 3 calendars. The next day, he spent another $18 for more calendars. Each calendar cost the same amount. How many calendars did Craig buy?

   _____

2. On Monday, Mrs. Jones spent $32 on 4 books. On Tuesday, she spent $16 on more books. Each book cost the same amount. How many books did Mrs. Jones buy?

   _____

3. Hailey spent $12 to buy 2 fish. Her cousin spent double the amount on fish. Each fish cost the same amount. How many fish do Hailey and her cousin have altogether?

   _____

4. **Write Math** ➤ **Explain** how you used the arrays to solve each problem.

   _____

   _____

Name _____

Search for Unknown Factors

**Find the unknown factor. Then write the word form of
the unknown factor on the line below the problem.**

1. [ ] $\times 7 = 35$

_____

2. [ ] $\times 7 = 7$

_____

3. $7 \times$ [ ] $= 70$

_____

4. [ ] $\times 7 = 63$

_____

5. [ ] $\times 7 = 0$

_____

6. [ ] $\times 7 = 56$

_____

7. [ ] $\times 7 = 42$

_____

8. [ ] $\times 7 = 28$

_____

9. [ ] $\times 7 = 14$

_____

10. [ ] $\times 7 = 49$

_____

**Find each word form for Exercises 1–10 in the word search
below. Words can be found written horizontally, vertically,
and diagonally, as well as forward and backward.**

F	I	V	E	T	O	X	E
O	W	N	H	M	W	I	I
Q	E	R	I	R	T	S	G
F	E	I	R	N	E	V	H
E	O	U	V	F	E	N	T
J	O	Y	T	E	N	M	O
F	I	N	E	V	E	S	N
F	Z	E	R	O	I	Z	T

Matching Factors and Products

Complete the number sentence in Column A. Then circle the correct product in Column B. In Column C, use 3 factors to write a number sentence for the product in Column B that is not circled.

Column A	Column B	Column C
1. $(9 \times 1) \times 2 = $ _____	18 14	
2. $7 \times (2 \times 3) = $ _____	42 16	
3. $8 \times (2 \times 2) = $ _____	48 32	
4. $(1 \times 2) \times 7 = $ _____	14 36	
5. $1 \times (3 \times 2) = $ _____	6 5	
6. $3 \times (8 \times 1) = $ _____	12 24	
7. $(3 \times 2) \times 6 = $ _____	36 40	
8. $(3 \times 3) \times 5 = $ _____	54 45	
9. $9 \times (3 \times 1) = $ _____	27 35	
10. $(7 \times 1) \times 4 = $ _____	60 28	

11. Write Math ▶ **Explain** how you decided which factors to group in Column C.

_____

Pattern Products

Follow the directions for the multiplication table.

1. Shade all of the products in the row and column for 2.

2. Circle all of the products in the row and column for 4.

3. Describe two patterns in the products that are shaded or circled.

_____

_____

_____

_____

×	0	1	2	3	4	5	6	7	8	9	10
0	0	0	0	0	0	0	0	0	0	0	0
1	0	1	2	3	4	5	6	7	8	9	10
2	0	2	4	6	8	10	12	14	16	18	20
3	0	3	6	9	12	15	18	21	24	27	30
4	0	4	8	12	16	20	24	28	32	36	40
5	0	5	10	15	20	25	30	35	40	45	50
6	0	6	12	18	24	30	36	42	48	54	60
7	0	7	14	21	28	35	42	49	56	63	70
8	0	8	16	24	32	40	48	56	64	72	80
9	0	9	18	27	36	45	54	63	72	81	90
10	0	10	20	30	40	50	60	70	80	90	100

4. **Write Math** ▶ Why are some numbers both shaded and circled?

_____

_____

5. **Stretch Your Thinking** Shade the row and column for 8. Compare the products to the products you have already shaded or circled. What patterns do you see?

_____

_____

_____

Name _____

Product Pyramids

The number in each box of a pyramid is the product of
the two numbers below it. Use multiplication to find the
missing numbers in each product pyramid.

1.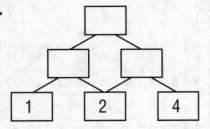

2.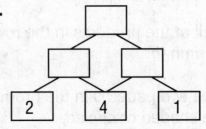

3.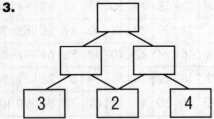

4.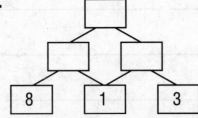

5.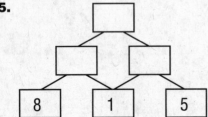

6.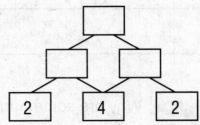

7.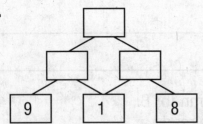

8.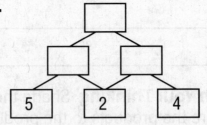

9. [Write Math] ▶ Haylie's work is shown
on the right. Is it correct? If not, find her
mistake and write a correct answer.

To find 8×9, I can find 4×9
then double the product.
$4 \times 9 = 32$
$32 + 32 = 64$
So, $8 \times 9 = 64$.

_____

_____

_____

Name _____

9s Riddle

Find each product. Then find the product in the code box. Write the code letter on the line above the exercise number at the bottom of the page. Then answer the mystery question.

CODE

A	C	D	E	F	H	M	N	O	R	S	T	V	W	Y
27	24	40	81	90	9	36	54	18	63	25	0	12	45	72

1. $9 \times 5 =$ _____

2. $3 \times 8 =$ _____

3. $0 \times 9 =$ _____

4. $5 \times 5 =$ _____

5. $9 \times 7 =$ _____

6. $3 \times 9 =$ _____

7. $9 \times 9 =$ _____

8. $10 \times 4 =$ _____

9. $6 \times 9 =$ _____

10. $4 \times 9 =$ _____

11. $9 \times 1 =$ _____

12. $4 \times 3 =$ _____

13. $8 \times 9 =$ _____

14. $2 \times 9 =$ _____

15. $9 \times 10 =$ _____

—— —— ——   —— —— —— ——
11   14   1   10   6   9   13

—— —— —— —— —— —— ——   —— —— —— ——
15   6   2   3   14   5   4   8   14   7   4

9 —— —— —— —— ? Answer _____
   11   6   12   7

Using Tables

Solve. Use a table to organize the information for 1–2.

1. Marcy uses 1 bottle of blue paint, 2 bottles of yellow paint, and 1 bottle of red paint for one painting. How many bottles of paint will she need to make 4 of the same paintings?

Number of Paintings	1			
Blue Paint	1			
Yellow Paint	2			
Red Paint	1			

_____

2. Miguel puts photos in an album. The album has 5 right-hand and 5 left-hand pages. Each right-hand page holds 4 photos. Each left-hand page holds 3 photos. How many photos will fit in the album?

Number of Pairs of Pages	1				
Right Page	4				
Left Page	3				

_____

3. Renee earns 2 dimes each time she helps her mother. How many dimes will she earn if she helps her mother 4 times a day for a week?

_____

4. Henry earns $6 every time he waters Mr. Young's lawn. How much will Henry earn if he waters the lawn 4 times in July and 4 times in August?

_____

5. **Stretch Your Thinking** Suppose Exercise 2 asked how many photos fit on the first 6 pages of Miguel's album. **Explain** how you could find the answer.

_____

_____

_____

Multistep Problems

Solve.

1. Keith bought 2 flats of strawberries. Each flat contains 8 baskets. If he gave away 4 baskets, how many baskets does Keith have left?

   _____

2. Tim's friends gave him $15 for pizza. If he buys 3 pizzas for $7 each, how much more money does Tim need?

   _____

3. One bag contains 6 apples. Jeremy bought 5 bags of apples. If Jeremy gave away 5 apples, how many apples does he have left?

   _____

4. Greeting cards come in packages of 8 cards for $4. How many greeting cards can Sheila buy for $24?

   _____

5. Anna is having a party. She needs 15 invitations. The invitations come in packages of 7. How many packages of invitations does Anna need to buy?

   _____

6. Steve is decorating for a party. He wants to have 2 blue balloons and 1 yellow balloon in each corner of a square room. How many balloons does Steve need?

   _____

7. **Write Math** ▸ **Explain** how you solved Problem 2.

   _____

   _____

   _____

   _____

Factor Riddles

Solve the riddles.

1. I have 4 factors. Three of my factors are 1, 2, and 10. What is my fourth factor?

   _____

2. I have 4 factors. Three of my factors are 1, 2, and 6. What is my fourth factor?

   _____

3. I am the product 30. Two of my factors are 2 and 3. What are my other factors?

   _____

4. Our product is equal to $3 + 3 + 3$. What factors are we?

   _____

5. Our product is equal to $6 + 2$. What factors are we?

   _____

6. One of my factors is equal to $5 - 2$. I am the product 24. What are my other factors?

   _____

7. I am a 2-digit product. One of my digits is the same as one of my factors, 8. The other digit doubled is 8. What product am I?

   _____

8. My product can be written using repeated addition as $5 + 5 + 5 + 5 + 5 + 5 + 5 + 5$. What are my factors?

   _____

9. **Write Math** ➤ **Explain** how you solved the riddle in Exercise 7.

   _____

   _____

   _____

10. **Stretch Your Thinking** Write your own riddle and solve it.

    _____

    _____

    _____

Apply the Distributive Property

Use the Distributive Property to help solve each problem.

Use this problem for 1–3.

An artist sells 4 paintings for $20 each, 4 sculptures for $60 each, and 4 photographs for $10 each at her art show.

Use this problem for 4–6.

Lee has 6 sheets of stickers with 30 stickers on each sheet. She has 8 sheets with 20 stickers each and 9 sheets with 10 stickers each.

1. How much money does the artist make on these sales in all?

   _____

2. The artist sells 2 more paintings and 4 more sculptures at the same prices. What is the total amount of money the artist has made so far?

   _____

3. How many more paintings, sculptures, and photographs would the artist need to sell to make another $500?

   _____

   _____

4. How many stickers does Lee have in all?

   _____

5. Lee gives 4 sheets with 20 stickers and 3 sheets with 10 stickers to her sister. How many stickers does Lee have left?

   _____

6. Now Lee gives some stickers to her friend Myla. What sheets does Lee give to Myla if she has 200 stickers left?

   _____

   _____

7. **Write Math** ▶ How did the Distributive Property help you solve the problems?

   _____

   _____

Name _____

Jump to the Product

**Complete the model to find the unknown factor or factors.
Then write a multiplication equation that represents the
model.**

1. The product is 80. One factor is 4.

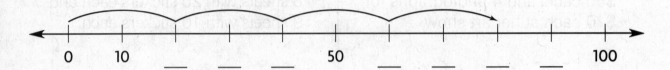

The unknown factor is _____. _____

2. The product is 180. One factor is a multiple of 10.

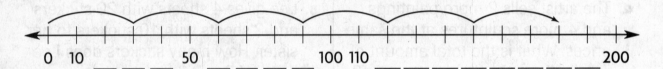

The factors are _____ and _____. _____

3. Stretch Your Thinking The product is 200. Both factors are
multiples of 10.

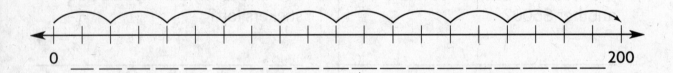

The factors are _____ and _____. _____

4. **Write Math** ► Look back at Exercise 2. If one factor is a multiple of 10, what
other pairs of factors would give you a product of 180?

_____

Multiplication Puzzle

Find the unknown factors and products. Then use your answers to complete the puzzle.

Across

1. $2 \times 70 = \blacksquare$

$\blacksquare =$ _____

2. $80 \times a = 240$

$a =$ _____

3. $b \times 80 = 720$

$b =$ _____

5. $60 \times c = 420$

$c =$ _____

7. $d \times 90 = 0$

$d =$ _____

Down

1. $2 \times 80 = \blacksquare$

$\blacksquare =$ _____

2. $p \times 1 = 30$

$p =$ _____

4. $8 \times q = 560$

$q =$ _____

6. $90 \times r = 360$

$r =$ _____

8. $s \times 9 = 810$

$s =$ _____

Modeling Problems

Model the problem to solve.

1. Gina needs to make 4 centerpieces with the same number of flowers in each centerpiece for the tables at her party. She bought 32 flowers to use. How many flowers will be in each centerpiece?

   _____

2. Gina bought 18 balloons. If she makes 3 equal groups of balloons, how many balloons will be in each group?

   _____

3. Gina bought 24 plates. If she stacks them in groups of 8, how many stacks of plates will she make?

   _____

4. There will be a total of 20 people at the party. There are 4 tables. If Gina wants an equal number of people at each table, how many chairs should she set at each table?

   _____

5. **Stretch Your Thinking** Find three more ways Gina could stack 24 plates into equal stacks, with at least 3 plates in a stack. Tell the number of stacks and how many would be in each stack.

   _____

   _____

Matching Models

Draw a line to match each word problem with the model you can use to solve it. Then write the answer.

1. Sean has 15 baseball cards. He puts them into equal groups. How many baseball cards does Sean put in each group?   •

A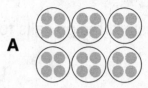

_____

2. Lucy has a box of 24 cookies. She divides them equally among some friends. How many cookies does each friend receive?   •

B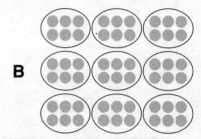

_____

3. Eddie has 56 coins in his collection. He separates the coins into equal groups. How many coins are in each group?   •

C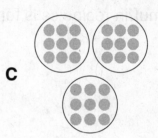

_____

4. Michael bought 54 juice boxes for a picnic. He plans to put an equal number at each of the picnic tables. How many juice boxes will Michael put at each table?   •

D

_____

5. Leona has 27 feathers to put on some masks. She uses the same number of feathers on each mask. How many feathers does she use on each mask?   •

E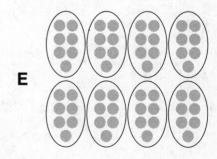

_____

Eggs in One Basket

For each of the following recipes, tell how many batches can be made using 24 eggs. Draw a quick picture with counters to solve each problem.

1. A custard recipe calls for 8 eggs.

2. An omelet recipe calls for 3 eggs.

_____

3. A muffin recipe calls for 2 eggs.

4. A French toast recipe calls for 12 eggs.

_____

5. Stretch Your Thinking If one batch of cookies calls for 5 eggs, how many batches can you make with 24 eggs? Will there be any eggs left over? **Explain.**

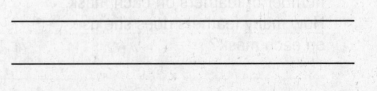

_____
_____
_____
_____

Name _____

Speedy Math

Solve each problem. For each exercise, the quotient has a matching letter. Place the letter above the exercise number to find the answer to the question.

1. 20 ÷ 5 = _____ 2. 42 ÷ 7 = _____

3. 25 ÷ 5 = _____ 4. 45 ÷ 9 = _____

5. 36 ÷ 4 = _____ 6. 12 ÷ 6 = _____

7. 48 ÷ 8 = _____

What is the fastest animal on land?

KEY	A	B	C	E	H	I	R	T
	2	3	4	5	6	7	8	9

_____ _____ _____ _____ _____ _____ _____
1. 2. 3. 4. 5. 6. 7.

8. **Stretch Your Thinking** Make up your own division exercises and puzzle to answer the question "What animal really likes carrots?" The answer is a "rabbit."

_____

_____

_____

Fish Tank Math

Jed works in a pet store that sells fish. He needs to move fish from the old tanks and put them in the new tanks. He can move the fish in small groups only.

Use repeated subtraction to solve each problem. Circle groups of fish each time you subtract. Then write how many equal groups Jed can make and how many fish are left over.

1. 19 ÷ 6

____ groups and ____ left over

2. 23 ÷ 5

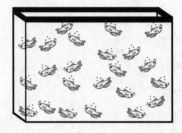

____ groups and ____ left over

3. 17 ÷ 3

____ groups and ____ left over

4. 15 ÷ 4

____ groups and ____ left over

5. Stretch Your Thinking Choose one of the problems. Change the number of fish in each group so there will not be any fish left over. **Explain** why you chose that tank.

_____

_____

_____

_____

Array Puzzles

Use the clues to help solve the puzzle. You can use tiles or draw the array on a separate sheet of paper.

1. I am an array made with 24 tiles. I have 8 tiles in each row. How many rows do I have?

   _____

2. I am an array with 4 equal rows. I have 16 tiles in all. How many tiles are in each of my rows?

   _____

3. I am a square-shaped array. I have 7 rows. How many tiles do I have in all? (Hint: A square has 4 sides of equal length.)

   _____

4. I am an array made with 24 tiles. My number of rows is 2 more than the number of tiles in each of my rows. How many rows do I have?

   _____

5. I am an array with 7 tiles in each row. My number of rows is 4 less than the number of tiles in each of my rows. How many tiles am I made with in all?

   _____

6. I am an array made with 40 tiles. I have an odd number of rows and an even number of tiles in each of my rows. The number of my rows plus the number of tiles in each of my rows equals 13. How many rows do I have?

   _____

7. **Write Math** ➤ Write your own array puzzle. Include the answer.

   _____

   _____

   _____

Multiplication and Division Match

Solve. Then draw a line to match each multiplication equation to a related division equation.

1. $2 \times 8 =$ _____ •

2. $5 \times 8 =$ _____ •

3. $3 \times 9 =$ _____ •

4. $6 \times 7 =$ _____ •

5. $2 \times 6 =$ _____ •

6. $5 \times 7 =$ _____ •

7. $6 \times 4 =$ _____ •

8. $8 \times 8 =$ _____ •

9. $3 \times 6 =$ _____ •

10. $9 \times 4 =$ _____ •

11. $9 \times 2 =$ _____ •

12. $8 \times 3 =$ _____ •

A $12 \div 2 = 6$

B $42 \div 7 = 6$

C $18 \div 3 = 6$

D $40 \div 8 = 5$

E $24 \div 6 = 4$

F $27 \div 9 = 3$

G $24 \div 3 = 8$

H $36 \div 9 = 4$

I $16 \div 2 = 8$

J $18 \div 2 = 9$

K $64 \div 8 = 8$

L $35 \div 5 = 7$

Related Fact Riddles

Related facts use three numbers. Solve each riddle to find the three numbers. Then, write the set of related facts for the numbers.

Remember the following vocabulary terms: *dividend ÷ divisor = quotient*.

1. Seven is the quotient. The dividend is a multiple of 3 that is less than 30.

_____

_____

2. The quotient is 7 less than the divisor. The dividend is 18.

_____

_____

3. This set of related facts contains two numbers less than 10. One of these numbers is the product of 3 and 3. When you multiply the two numbers, the product is a multiple of 5. Write the related facts.

_____

_____

4. The quotient and the divisor are the same number. The sum is 8. Write the related facts.

_____

_____

5. **Write Math** ▶ How many equations did you write for Exercise 4? How do you know your answer is correct?

_____

_____

6. Stretch Your Thinking Write a riddle for three numbers in a set of related facts. Then write the related facts for the numbers.

_____

_____

_____

A Planet of 1 and 0

**Fill in the correct quotient to complete the fact.
Then, fill in the other blank with the word that makes the
most sense from the box below. Each word may be used
only once. Some words will not be used.**

planets	kite	letter
toes		
rock	cities	

1. On the Earth's surface, there are _____ basic types of _____.
   (3 ÷ 1)

2. The number _____ looks like the _____ O.
   (0 ÷ 4)

3. There are usually _____ fingers and _____ on each hand
   and foot.   (5 ÷ 1)

4. In our solar system, _____ of the _____, Mercury and Venus,
   have no moons.   (2 ÷ 1)

5. **Stretch Your Thinking** If Exercise 2 had read 4 ÷ 0,
   could it be solved? **Explain**.

   _____

   _____

6. **Write Math** ➤ Write a fill-in story like the exercises above, using
   a rule for 1 or 0. Use one of the words left in the box.

   _____

   _____

   _____

Division Maze

Begin at START and find your way through the maze. Follow only numbers that can be divided by 2 with none left over. End at FINISH.

START 2	67	40	13	17	67	9
13	10	71	22	33	91	19
49	11	49	17	66	81	93
101	23	39	311	47	16	113
53	1	51	3	46	31	21
24 FINISH	42	12	38	7	1	19

1. **Write Math** How did you know which number to go to next after the digit 2 in the START space? **Explain.**

   _____

   _____

2. **Stretch Your Thinking** How many numbers from 1 through 100 can be divided by 2 with none left over? Are the numbers *even* or *odd*?

   _____

© Houghton Mifflin Harcourt Publishing Company

Olympics Math

A decade is equal to 10 years.

Use the table for 1–3.

Summer Olympics	
Year	Location
1996	Atlanta, United States
2000	Sydney, Australia
2004	Athens, Greece
2008	Beijing, China
2012	London, Great Britain

1. The 1992 Summer Olympics were held in Barcelona, Spain. How many decades later will the Summer Olympics be held in London, Great Britain?

_____

2. The 1960 Summer Olympics were held in Rome, Italy. How many decades later were the Summer Olympics held in Sydney, Australia?

_____

3. The Summer Olympics were held in St. Louis 92 years before the Summer Olympics were held in Atlanta. In what year were the Olympics held in St. Louis?

_____

4. The 1932 Summer Olympics were held in Los Angeles. Seven decades later the Winter Olympics were held in Salt Lake City. In what year were the Winter Olympics held in Salt Lake City?

_____

5. **Write Math** ▶ Harrison was born in 2003. How many decades old will he be in 2023? **Explain** how you found your answer.

_____

_____

6. **Stretch Your Thinking** Look at the Summer Olympics table above. After the 2012 Olympics, what year will be the next time the Summer Olympics are held? **Explain.**

_____

_____

Divide by 5 to Guess My Number

Read the clues. Use all the clues to guess the number.

1. I am a 1-digit number. I am not even. If you multiply me by 10, then divide the answer by 5, the quotient is 6. What number am I?

   _____

2. If you divide me by 2 and then multiply the answer by 10, you get a product of 20. What number am I?

   _____

3. If you multiply me by 2, then divide the answer by 2, then divide again by 2, you get a quotient of 5. What number am I?

   _____

4. I am a 2-digit number. If you divide me by 5, then multiply me by 2, the product is 20. What number am I?

   _____

5. I am the number of tiles in a tile design. Each tile in the design has 5 sides. There are 40 sides on the tiles in all. What number am I?

   _____

6. I am the number of red tiles in a design with red and blue tiles. The red tiles each have 3 sides. The blue tiles each have 5 sides. There are 3 blue tiles. There are 30 sides on the tiles in all. What number am I?

   _____

7. **Write Math** ► Write a problem like the ones on this page. Include multiplication and division in your clues. Exchange your problem with a partner and solve.

   _____

   _____

   _____

Three's Teams

The community center is organizing three teams for each of the sports they offer. The number of people on each of the 3 teams for each sport is listed below. Tell how many players have signed up for each sport in all. Then tell how you could organize the teams so each one has the same number of players.

1. Tennis: 2, 4, 3

_____

_____

2. Golf: 2, 4, 6

_____

_____

3. Soccer: 8, 10, 9

_____

_____

4. Baseball: 9, 7, 8

_____

_____

5. **Write Math** ▸ The 3 teams for basketball had 5 people, 7 people, and 9 people. How many people will be on the 3 equal teams for basketball? **Explain.**

_____

_____

_____

6. Stretch Your Thinking The 3 teams for football had 15, 12, and 27 people. How many people will be on 3 equal teams for football? **Explain** how you found your answer.

_____

_____

_____

Count the Signs

Arial, Brian, and Craig are playing a game. Arial gets a point every time the answer to a problem is =. Brian gets a point every time the answer is <, and Craig gets a point when it is >. Write <, >, or =. Keep track of each player's points.

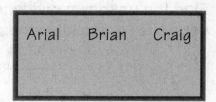

Arial   Brian   Craig

1. $2 \times 8 \bigcirc 24 \div 4$

2. $36 - 15 \bigcirc 3 \times 7$

3. $16 \div 4 \bigcirc 8 + 5$

4. $2 \times 8 \bigcirc 24 \div 3$

5. $36 \div 4 \bigcirc 1 \times 9$

6. $28 - 15 \bigcirc 30 \div 3$

7. $17 + 8 \bigcirc 6 \times 6$

8. $3 \times 3 \bigcirc 18 \div 2$

9. $28 \div 4 \bigcirc 16 \div 2$

10. $11 + 9 \bigcirc 4 \times 5$

11. $0 + 7 \bigcirc 32 \div 4$

12. $2 \times 7 \bigcirc 12 \div 3$

13. $20 \div 4 \bigcirc 15 \div 3$

14. $27 \div 3 \bigcirc 54 - 45$

15. **Write Math** ▶ Who won the game? **Explain.**

_____

_____

16. **Stretch Your Thinking** Drew asks if he can play the game. He wants to use the sign ≠ (is not equal to). How many points would Drew get for ≠? **Explain.**

_____

_____

_____

Name _____

Division Puzzle

Find the unknown dividends and quotients. Then use
your answers to fill in the puzzle.

Across

1. $60 \div 6 =$ _____

2. $6 \div 6 =$ _____

3. $24 \div 6 =$ _____

4. _____ $\div 4 = 12 - 3$

5. $42 \div 6 =$ _____

8. _____ $\div 6 = 9$

10. $12 \div 6 =$ _____

Down

1. _____ $\div 2 = 4 + 5$

2. _____ $\div 4 = 8 \div 2$

4. $18 \div 6 =$ _____

6. _____ $\div 4 = 2 \times 4$

7. _____ $\div 6 = 5$

9. _____ $\div 6 = 8$

11. Write Math ▶ How did you find the dividend for 9 Down?

_____

_____

Monster Ball

**The monsters at the ball had different numbers of feet.
Here is a list of the different monsters at the ball.**

biped	triped	quadruped	pentaped	hexaped	septaped
2 feet	3 feet	4 feet	5 feet	6 feet	7 feet

1. A group of quadrupeds were standing together. There were a total of 20 feet. How many quadrupeds were in the group?

_____

2. A group of septapeds were standing together. There were a total of 42 feet. How many septapeds were in the group?

_____

3. There were 2 hexapeds and 4 tripeds dancing. How many feet were dancing?

_____

4. A group of septapeds and 3 bipeds were dancing. There were a total of 41 feet. How many septapeds were in the group?

_____

5. **Write Math** ➤ Write and solve a word problem about the monsters at the ball.

_____

_____

_____

6. **Stretch Your Thinking** A group of bipeds and pentapeds were standing together. There were a total of 33 feet. How many bipeds and pentapeds can be standing in the group? **Explain.**

_____

_____

Space Weight

**Weight is the measure of how heavy an object is. The
weight of an object on Earth is about 8 times as great as
that object's weight on Callisto, a moon of Jupiter. For each
object below, write a division equation to find the weight
on Callisto.**

1. A 16-pound cat

_____

2. A 56-pound dog

_____

3. A 40-pound suitcase

_____

4. A 48-pound child

_____

5. An 80-pound machine

_____

6. A 160-pound man

_____

7. Write Math ➤ The weight of an object on Earth is about
6 times as great as the object's weight on Earth's moon.
What is the weight of an object on Earth's moon if it
weighs 42 pounds on Earth? **Explain.**

_____

_____

_____

8. Stretch Your Thinking An object would weigh 6 pounds
on Callisto. What would it weigh on Earth's moon? **Explain.**

_____

_____

_____

Left Overs

Complete the table.

	Counters	How many in each group?	How many equal groups?	How many left over?
1.	14	4		
2.	15	4		
3.	16	4		
4.	45	8		
5.	46	8		
6.	26	7		
7.	27	7		
8.	25	9		
9.	26	9		

10. **Write Math** ▶ What are all the possible remainders (number left over) when you divide a number by 9? **Explain**.

_____

_____

_____

11. **Stretch Your Thinking** You divide a number and get a remainder of 4. What 1-digit number can be the divisor of the problem? **Explain**.

_____

_____

_____

Division Steps

Solve. Show your steps to find the answer.

1. Veronica bought a pack of 50 CDs. She gave 8 to her friend, Leslie. Then she made 6 equal sets of CDs. How many CDs are in each set?

   _____

   _____

2. Sid has 2 boxes of markers with the same number of markers in each box. He gives 3 markers to his sister. Now Sid has 13 markers. How many markers were in each box?

   _____

   _____

3. Casey bought 30 basketball trading cards. He gave 6 to his sister and then put the rest in an album. If 6 cards fit on one page of the album, how many pages did Casey use?

   _____

   _____

4. Barron bought a 25-pound bag of dog food. He still had 3 pounds from an older bag. If he feeds his dogs 4 pounds of food each week, how many weeks until all the dog food is gone?

   _____

   _____

5. Manny ordered 16 skateboard wheels. If he sold 4 wheels to Brad, how many skateboards can he put wheels on if each board uses 4 wheels?

   _____

   _____

6. Kiera has 27 balls of yarn. Her mother gave her 5 more balls. If she makes scarves that use 4 balls each, how many scarves can she make?

   _____

   _____

7. **Write Math** ▸ Thomas starts with 36 photos and throws away 6 that are too dark. Then he organizes the rest of them on scrapbook pages so that there are 5 photos on each page. How many pages will he use? Draw to **explain**.

   _____

Order of Operations

Find the unknown number that makes the equation true.
Follow the order of operations.

1. $2 + 3 \times \blacksquare = 20$

_____

2. $12 \div \blacksquare - 2 = 2$

_____

3. $4 \times 6 - \blacksquare = 12$

_____

4. $\blacksquare + 6 \times 3 = 20$

_____

5. $5 + \blacksquare \div 6 = 8$

_____

6. $20 - \blacksquare \div 8 = 18$

_____

7. $14 - 2 \times \blacksquare = 0$

_____

8. $30 \div 6 \times \blacksquare = 45$

_____

9. $9 \times \blacksquare - 20 = 16$

_____

10. $\blacksquare + 2 \times 5 = 45$

_____

11. $\blacksquare + 24 \div 4 = 7$

_____

12. $9 + 7 - \blacksquare = 11$

_____

7. **Write Math** ▶ **Explain** how you found the unknown number in Exercise 9.

_____

_____

_____

_____

Way to Share!

**Draw lines to divide each shape 3 different ways
into the number of parts given.**

1. 4 equal parts

2. 3 equal parts

3. 6 equal parts

4. **Write Math** ▶ Look back at Exercise 1. How did you decide
where to divide each square?

_____

_____

5. **Stretch Your Thinking** How do you know the square is divided
into equal parts even though they are not the same shape?

_____

_____

_____

A Fair Share

Mary and her 3 friends go on a picnic. They share some food. Show how they can make the fewest cuts possible to share the food equally among 4 people. Shade your drawing to show one person's share. Then write how much each person gets.

1. 4 sandwiches

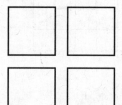

_____

2. 2 muffins

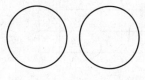

_____

3. 3 small pizzas

_____

4. 6 granola bars

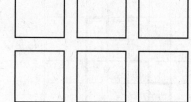

_____

5. **Write Math** ▶ How can you tell if an equal share is more than one whole? Use an example from above to explain your answer.

_____

_____

_____

_____

Name _____

Whole Lot of Fractions!

Draw lines and shade each shape to show the fraction.

1. $\frac{1}{2}$
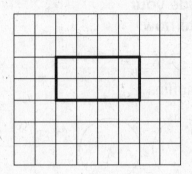

2. $\frac{1}{4}$
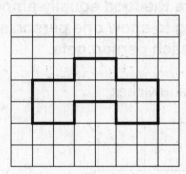

3. $\frac{1}{4}$

4. $\frac{1}{8}$
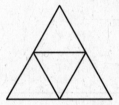

5. $\frac{1}{3}$
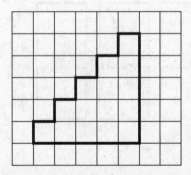

6. $\frac{1}{2}$
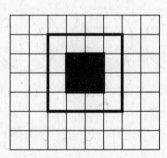

7. **Stretch Your Thinking** What unit fraction of the figure is shaded? **Explain** your answer.

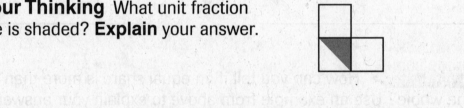

_____

_____

Name _____

Flag Fractions

Write a fraction to name the shaded part of each flag.

1.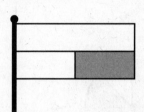

_____

2.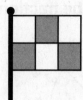

_____

3.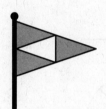

_____

4.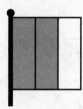

_____

5.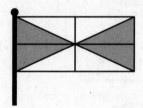

_____

6.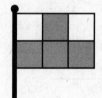

_____

7. **Write Math** ▸ Draw your own flag. Divide it into equal parts. Shade some of the equal parts. Then write the fraction that names the shaded part of your flag.

_____

Fraction Find

Write a fraction that names the shaded part of
each whole. Then locate the fraction on the
number line below. Write the letter of the model
that represents the fraction.

A.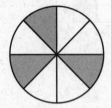

B.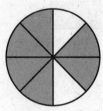

_____   _____

C.

D.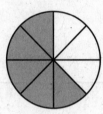

_____   _____

E.

F.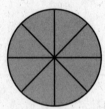

_____   _____

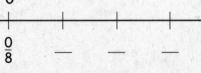

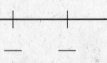

Fraction and Whole Number Match

For each model, write a fraction greater than 1 for the parts that are shaded. Then, for 1–3, write the letter of the model below the dashed line that shows the same whole number.

1.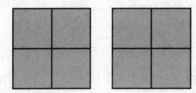

_____ _____

2.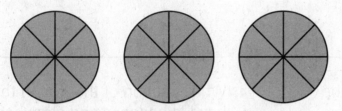

_____ _____

3.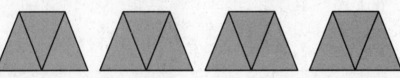

_____ _____

- -

A.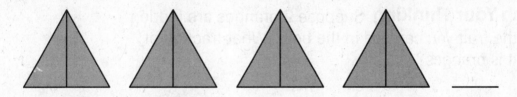

_____

B.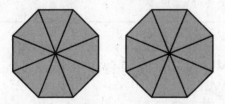

_____

C.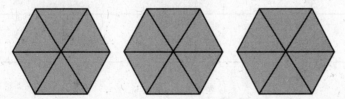

_____

Fruit Fractions

Use the bowl of fruit to answer the questions.
The bowl has 3 strawberries, 2 bananas,
and 1 apple.

1. What fraction of the fruit in the
bowl is bananas?

_____

2. What fraction of the fruit in the
bowl is apples?

_____

3. What fraction of the fruit in the
bowl is strawberries?

_____

4. What fraction of the fruit in the
bowl is bananas and strawberries?

_____

5. Stretch Your Thinking Suppose 2 oranges are hidden
under the fruit you can see in the bowl. What fraction of
the fruit is oranges?

_____

6. **Write Math** ▶ Write your own problem about fractions of a group.
Use the fruit in the bowl. Then write the answer.

_____

_____

_____

Part of the Group

Evan and his friends go to a theme park. Each friend buys 24 tickets and rides only 1 ride. Solve the problem.

1. Evan uses $\frac{1}{3}$ of his tickets to ride the Loop-D-Loop. How many tickets does he use?

   _____

2. Omar uses $\frac{1}{6}$ of his tickets to ride the water slide. How many tickets does he use?

   _____

3. Kate uses $\frac{1}{2}$ of her tickets to ride the roller coaster. How many tickets does she use?

   _____

4. Jenny uses $\frac{1}{4}$ of her tickets to ride the merry-go-round. How many tickets does she use?

   _____

5. **Stretch Your Thinking** Use the information in 1–4 to find the number of tickets each friend has left.

Name	Number of Tickets Left
Evan	
Omar	
Kate	
Jenny	

6. **Write Math** ➤ The friends now want to go on the Loop-D-Loop and the roller coaster. Explain why only 1 of the friends can go on both of these rides.

   _____

   _____

   _____

What Part of the Group?

Draw a quick picture to solve.

1. Lisa's dog has 4 squeaky toys. Two thirds of the dog's toys are squeaky toys. How many dog toys does Lisa's dog have in all?

2. Sam has 9 yellow pencils in his desk. Three fourths of his pencils are yellow. How many pencils does Sam have in his desk?

_____

_____

3. Julia has 8 red barrettes. Two fourths of her barrettes are red. How many barrettes does Julia have?

4. Antonio has 15 pennies in his pocket. Five eighths of his coins are pennies. How many coins does Antonio have in his pocket?

_____

_____

5. **Stretch Your Thinking** One half of the birds at a pet store are yellow. Tara buys one of the yellow birds. Then one third of the birds at the store are yellow. How many yellow birds were at the pet store before Tara bought one? **Explain** how you know.

_____

_____

_____

Fraction Frenzy

Use the model to help you compare the fractions.
Write < or > .

1. Compare $\frac{3}{8}$ and $\frac{7}{8}$.

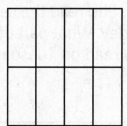

$\frac{3}{8} \bigcirc \frac{7}{8}$

2. Compare $\frac{2}{6}$ and $\frac{5}{6}$.

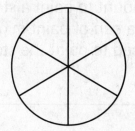

$\frac{2}{6} \bigcirc \frac{5}{6}$

3. Compare $\frac{1}{2}$ and $\frac{1}{4}$.

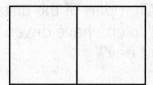

$\frac{1}{2} \bigcirc \frac{1}{4}$

4. **Write Math** ▶ Draw a set of 8 counters and color $\frac{4}{8}$ of the counters red. Draw another set of 8 counters and color $\frac{5}{8}$ red. Write < or > to compare the fraction of red counters in the two sets.

$\frac{4}{8} \bigcirc \frac{5}{8}$

Name _____

More or Less

**Write all the fractions with the same denominator
that can answer the question.**

1. Susan ate part of a pizza. She ate more than $\frac{1}{3}$ of the pizza. How much of the pizza might Susan have eaten?

   _____

2. Jean read $\frac{1}{4}$ of her book on Monday. She read the same amount on Tuesday. What part of her book did Jean read on Tuesday?

   _____

3. Amy began a running program. She ran less than $\frac{5}{6}$ of a mile. What part of a mile could Amy have run?

   _____

4. Alex used $\frac{3}{8}$ of a can of paint to paint a chair. He used less than that amount to paint a stool. What part of a can of paint might Alex have used to paint the stool?

   _____

5. Paul practiced playing the piano for $\frac{1}{2}$ hour on Friday. He practiced for the same amount of time on Saturday. How long did Paul practice on Saturday?

   _____

6. Jolene drove to a state park. She drove $\frac{1}{4}$ of the distance the first day. She drove farther the second day. What part of the distance might Jolene have driven the second day?

   _____

7. **Write Math** ▸ **Explain** how you solved Exercise 6.

   _____

   _____

   _____

   _____

Spin the Wheel of Fractions

Use the spinners for 1–6.

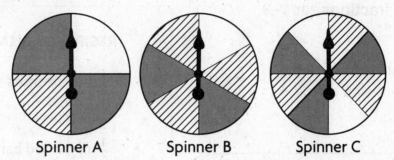

Spinner A   Spinner B   Spinner C

1. Use fractions to compare the white section on Spinner A to the white section on Spinner B.

_____

2. Use fractions to compare the striped sections on Spinner B to the striped sections on Spinner C.

_____

3. Use fractions to compare the gray sections on Spinner B to the gray sections on Spinner A.

_____

4. Use fractions to compare the gray sections on Spinner B to the white sections on Spinner C.

_____

5. Use fractions to compare the striped section and white section combined on Spinner A to the gray sections on Spinner A.

_____

6. Use fractions to compare the white sections on Spinner C to the gray sections on Spinner A.

_____

7. **Stretch Your Thinking** Draw two spinners that are the same size. Divide each spinner into a different number of equal parts. Color two parts on each spinner red. Then use fractions to compare the red parts on your spinners.

Food Fractions

Use the recipe for 1–6. Write a comparison statement with fractions for 1–3.

<table>
<tr><td colspan="2">

RECIPE FOR SNACK MIX

$\frac{2}{3}$ cup peanuts

$\frac{1}{2}$ cup pretzels

$\frac{1}{4}$ cup dried bananas

$\frac{1}{3}$ cup cereal squares

$\frac{3}{4}$ cup raisins

</td></tr>
</table>

1. Is a lesser amount of dried bananas or raisins used?

_____

2. Is a greater amount of raisins or peanuts used?

_____

3. Is a greater amount of cereal squares or pretzels used?

_____

4. Which ingredient has the least amount in the recipe?

_____

5. Which ingredient has the greatest amount in the recipe?

_____

6. What if $\frac{2}{2}$ cup of chocolate chips is added to the recipe? Would there be a greater amount of pretzels or chocolate chips?

_____

7. **Write Math** ► Make up your own recipe or find one at home. Then compare some of the amounts of ingredients.

_____

_____

_____

Race to the Fraction Line

Use the table for 1–7.

Race Results					
Runners	Jean	Shannon	Sally	Julie	Rachel
Fraction of Race Completed After 30 Minutes	$\frac{3}{8}$	$\frac{3}{4}$	$\frac{1}{4}$	$\frac{2}{4}$	$\frac{5}{8}$

1. Who is closest to the finish line? What fraction of the race has she run?

_____

2. Who is farthest from the finish line?

_____

3. List Jean, Shannon, and Sally in order from the closest to the finish line to the farthest.

_____

4. List Shannon, Julie, and Rachel in order from the farthest from the finish line to the closest.

_____

5. List all the fractions of the race completed in order from closest to the finish line to the farthest.

_____

6. List all the runners in order from farthest from the finish line to the closest.

_____

_____

7. **Write Math** Ashley is another runner, and she has completed $\frac{7}{8}$ of the race. Is she closest to the finish line? **Explain** your answer.

_____

_____

Name _____

Name Equivalent Fractions

For each of the following shapes, shade some of the parts. Write the fraction that represents the parts you shaded. Then use the shape to write an equivalent fraction for the parts you shaded.

1.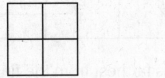

Fraction: _____

Equivalent Fraction: _____

2.

Fraction: _____

Equivalent Fraction: _____

3.

Fraction: _____

Equivalent Fraction: _____

4.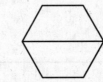

Fraction: _____

Equivalent Fraction: _____

5.

Fraction: _____

Equivalent Fraction: _____

6.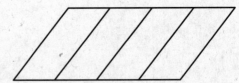

Fraction: _____

Equivalent Fraction: _____

7. **Stretch Your Thinking** Draw a model that shows $\frac{3}{3}$ shaded.

Then use your drawing to find two equivalent fractions.

Fractions Equal Fun

Use equivalent fractions and the information in the table for 1–6.

Marble Collections				
Friend	Steve	Kim	Mary	Damon
Fraction of Marbles That Are a Solid Color	$\frac{1}{8}$	$\frac{2}{3}$	$\frac{1}{6}$	$\frac{3}{4}$
Fraction of Marbles That Are Striped	$\frac{7}{8}$	$\frac{1}{3}$	$\frac{5}{6}$	$\frac{1}{4}$

1. If Steve has 16 marbles, how many are a solid color?

2. If Damon has 20 marbles altogether, how many of them are striped?

3. If Kim has 12 solid-color marbles, how many marbles does she have altogether?

4. If Mary has 10 striped marbles, how many marbles does she have altogether?

5. **What if** Mary has 15 striped marbles? How many solid-color marbles does she have?

6. If Steve has 4 solid-color marbles, how many marbles does he have altogether?

7. **Stretch Your Thinking** Ann arranges her marbles in groups, with 8 marbles in each group. She writes the fraction $\frac{5}{8}$ to show the fraction of marbles in each group that is red. What equivalent fraction names the fraction of marbles in 6 groups that are red? **Explain**.

Name _____

Time Tester

Solve the problem using the digital clock shown. Then use the analog clock at the right of the digital clock to show your answer.

1. Andy ate breakfast when his clock had the time shown. The clock stopped 12 minutes before breakfast. What time did Andy eat breakfast?

_____

2. Tyler left math class 23 minutes before the time shown. What time did Tyler leave math class?

_____

3. Larry knows he has recess 14 minutes after the time shown. What time does Larry have recess?

_____

4. **Stretch Your Thinking** Renee arrived at school at the time shown. The clock at school was 4 minutes fast. What time was shown on the clock at school when Renee arrived?

_____

Time Order

Use A.M. or P.M. to write the time for each activity below. Then write the sequence, or order, of the times from A.M. to P.M.

1.

_____   _____   _____   _____

go to sleep   ride the bus   do homework   take guitar lesson
                     to school

A.M. to P.M. in order:

_____   _____   _____   _____

2.

_____   _____   _____   _____

eat dinner   begin gym class   wake up   go to the library

A.M. to P.M. in order:

_____   _____   _____   _____

3. **Write Math** ▸ **Explain** how you found the order of the times in Exercise 2.

_____

_____

_____

_____

How Much Time?

Find the elapsed time.

1. Mia's soccer practice started at 3:15 P.M. and ended at 4:10 P.M. How long was Mia's soccer practice?

_____

2. Alex started eating lunch at 1:20 P.M. He finished at 1:55 in the afternoon. How long did it take Alex to eat lunch?

_____

3. Rose started eating breakfast at 7:45 in the morning. She finished at 8:35. How long did it take for Rose to eat breakfast?

_____

4. Jackson went outside to look at the stars at 8:40 in the evening. He went back inside at 9:25 P.M. How long did Jackson look at the stars?

_____

5. Julio started his homework at 4:40 in the afternoon. He finished at 5:05 P.M. How long did it take Julio to finish his homework?

_____

6. **Stretch Your Thinking** Pilar wakes up at 6:45 A.M. If she eats breakfast 15 minutes later, at what time does Pilar eat breakfast?

_____

Missing Times

Find the missing times to complete the table.

	Starting Time	Ending Time	Elapsed Time
1.	4:15 P.M.		45 minutes
2.		12:45 P.M.	95 minutes
3.		2:45 P.M.	61 minutes
4.	3:45 A.M.		75 minutes
5.	8:32 A.M.		30 minutes
6.		7:25 P.M.	100 minutes
7.		8:37 P.M.	153 minutes
8.	12:35 P.M.		45 minutes
9.		1:33 A.M.	250 minutes
10.	3:13 P.M.		120 minutes
11.		12:17 P.M.	15 minutes

12. **Stretch Your Thinking** What would be the Ending Time
in Exercise 10 if the Elapsed Time were 360 minutes?
Explain how you found your answer.

_____

_____

_____

Name _____

Spending Time at Camp

Tomas has to make a schedule for a day at camp. Use the information below to make a possible schedule that includes each activity. Use the number line to show when each activity will happen.

1. Breakfast starts at 8:00 A.M. and lasts for 30 minutes.

2. Lunch lasts 45 minutes and ends at 12:15 P.M.

3. The day at camp ends after lunch at 12:15 P.M.

4. Sports last 60 minutes.

5. Craft class starts right after breakfast and lasts 45 minutes.

6. Fishing lessons last 30 minutes.

7. Nature walk lasts 45 minutes and ends before sports.

8:00 A.M.   12:15 P.M.

8. How long is a day at camp? Write the elapsed time.

_____

9. **Stretch Your Thinking** Use the schedule and your number line. Can fishing happen before the nature walk? **Explain**.

_____

_____

_____

Measurement Hunt

Use a ruler to find objects that match each measure.
Write the name of each object to complete the table.

	Nearest Half Inch	Object	Nearest Fourth Inch	Object
1.	$1\frac{1}{2}$		$1\frac{1}{4}$	
2.	$2\frac{1}{2}$		$2\frac{1}{4}$	
3.	$3\frac{1}{2}$		$3\frac{1}{4}$	
4.	$4\frac{1}{2}$		$4\frac{3}{4}$	
5.	5		$5\frac{1}{4}$	
6.	$6\frac{1}{2}$		$6\frac{3}{4}$	
7.	$7\frac{1}{2}$		$7\frac{1}{4}$	
8.	$8\frac{1}{2}$		$8\frac{1}{4}$	
9.	9		9	

10. **Write Math** ▶ How did you identify objects to match each measure? **Explain.**

_____

_____

_____

_____

Estimate Liquid Volumes

**Choose a container that you estimate will have the liquid
volume given when the container is filled. Draw and label
the container you chose.**

Liquid Volume	Container
1. less than 1 liter	
2. about 1 liter	
3. more than 1 liter	

5. **Write Math** ▶ How did you decide what container to choose
for each liquid volume? **Explain.**

_____

_____

_____

Balancing Act

**Look at the object on the left pan of the balance in
Column A. Find the object in Column B you would
put on the right pan to make the pans balance.**

Column A	**Column B**

1. 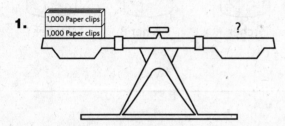 ___ **A.**

2. 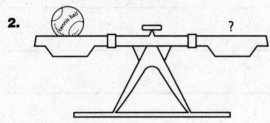 ? ___ **B.**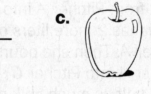

3. 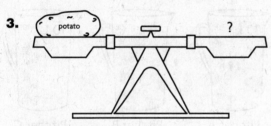 ? ___ **C.**

4. 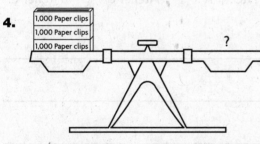 ? ___ **D.**

5. **Write Math** ▶ **Explain** how you decided which objects
have the same mass.

_____

_____

_____

Name _____

Pitcher Perfect

Solve the problem.

1. Kayla pours juice from Pitcher *A* into Pitcher *B* until both have the same amount of juice. Then she pours juice from Pitchers *A* and *B* into Pitcher *C* until all three pitchers have the same amount of juice. How many liters of juice will be in each pitcher? Explain.

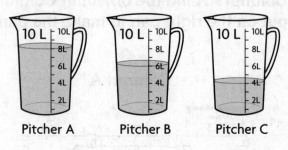

Pitcher A   Pitcher B   Pitcher C

_____

_____

_____

_____

2. Kirit pours milk from Pitcher *A* into Pitcher *B* until it has 2 more liters of milk than Pitcher *A*. Then she pours milk from Pitcher *A* into Pitcher *C* until it has one-half as much milk as Pitcher *B*. How many liters of milk does Kirit pour into Pitcher *C*? Explain.

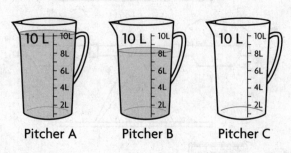

Pitcher A   Pitcher B   Pitcher C

_____

_____

_____

3. **Stretch Your Thinking** Describe another way to fill Pitcher *C* to get the same amount as in Problem 2.

_____

_____

Name _____

Draw Your Perimeter

Use the grid to draw two different shapes that have the given perimeter.

1. 16 units

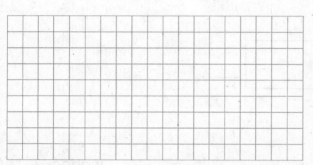

2. 24 units

3. 28 units

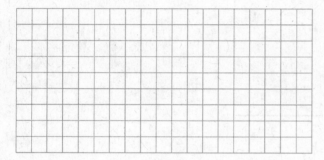

4. 30 units

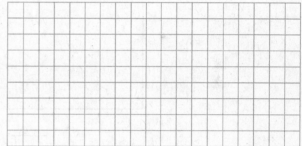

5. **Write Math** Eduardo drew a shape that had a perimeter of 20 units. The length of each side was 5 units. What shape could Eduardo have drawn? **Explain**.

_____

_____

_____

Find My Perimeter

Measure each side to the nearest $\frac{1}{2}$ inch.
Then find the perimeter of each shape.
(Hint: $\frac{1}{2} + \frac{1}{2} = 1$).

1.

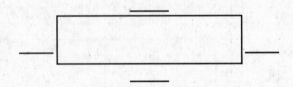

_____ in. + _____ in. + _____ in. + _____ in. = _____ inches

2.

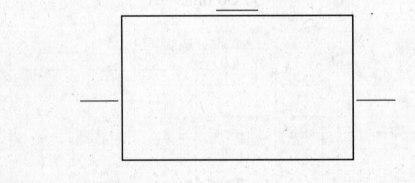

_____ in. + _____ in. + _____ in. + _____ in. = _____ inches

3. **Write Math** ▶ **Explain** how you added the measurements in
Exercise 2 to find the perimeter.

_____

_____

_____

_____

Perimeter Reasoning

Find and label the length of each unknown side.

1. Perimeter = 12 meters

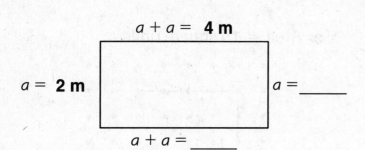

2. Perimeter = 24 feet

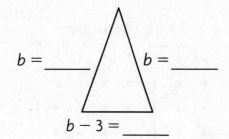

3. Perimeter = 30 meters

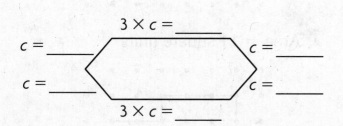

4. Perimeter = 48 yards

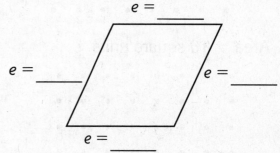

5. Perimeter = 10 feet

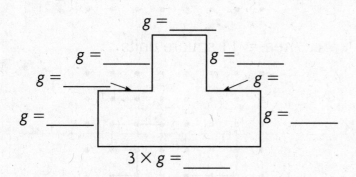

6. Perimeter = 35 yards

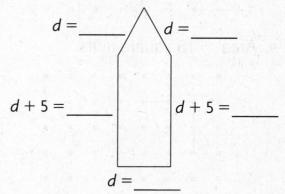

Connect the Dots to Show the Area

On each piece of dot paper below, a shape has been started.
Use the area to complete the shape by connecting the dots.
Connect the dots to complete the shape with the given area.

1. Area = 11 square units

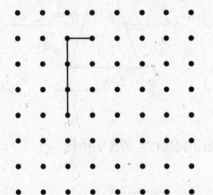

2. Area = 15 square units

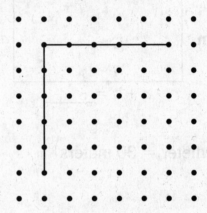

3. Area = 16 square units

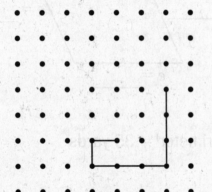

4. Area = 11 square units

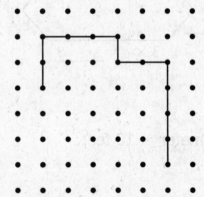

5. Area = 13 square units

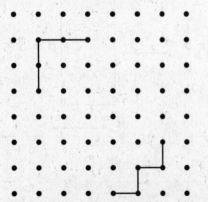

6. Area = 11 square units

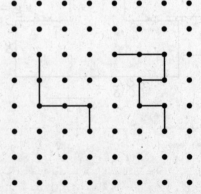

Name _____

Find Area

Find the area of each shape.
1 unit square is 1 square centimeter. (Hint: two half-unit squares
make one unit square.)

1.

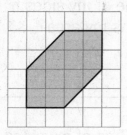

Area = _____ square centimeters

2.

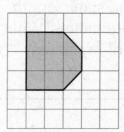

Area = _____ square centimeters

3.

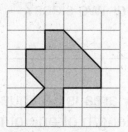

Area = _____ square centimeters

4.

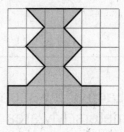

Area = _____ square centimeters

5.

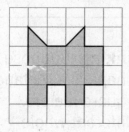

Area = _____ square centimeters

6.

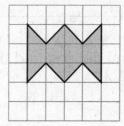

Area = _____ square centimeters

7. **Write Math** ▶ How did you find the area in Exercise 6?

_____

_____

_____

Area Riddles

Use the clues to solve the riddle.
You may use grid paper to draw the shape.

1. My sides are all the same length. My area is 9 square meters. What is the length of one of my sides?

_____

2. I am a square. One of my sides is 9 feet long. What is my area?

_____

3. I am a rectangle. One of my sides is 8 centimeters long. Another side is 6 centimeters long. What is my area?

_____

4. I am a rectangle. Two of my sides are each 7 inches long. My area is 28 square inches. What is the length of each of my other two sides?

_____

5. I am a rectangle. Each of my shorter sides measure 5 meters. My area is 45 square meters. What is the length of each of my longer sides?

_____

6. I am a square. My area is 64 square feet. What is the length of one of my sides?

_____

7. **Write Math** How did you find the answer in Exercise 4?

_____

_____

8. **Stretch Your Thinking** Suppose you know that a shape is a rectangle and its area is 8 square meters. What are all the different whole-number side lengths the rectangle could have?

_____

_____

Name _____

Find the Missing Information

Use the given information to find the missing information in the problem. Write the missing information. Then solve the problem.

1. Kelly builds a dog run that is 3 feet wide and has an area

of 12 square feet. The length of the dog run is _____ feet.
Kelly's brother builds another dog run that is also
3 feet wide, but its area is double that of Kelly's dog run.
What is the length of Kelly's brother's dog run?

_____ feet

2. Mrs. Thompson builds a vegetable garden that is
10 meters long and has an area of 40 square meters.

The width of the vegetable garden is _____ meters.
She also builds an herb garden that has the same width,
but its area is half that of her vegetable garden. What is
the length of Mrs. Thompson's herb garden?

_____ meters

3. Duane builds a square snow fort that is 4 feet long on

each side. The area of his snow fort is _____ square feet.
He then builds a second snow fort that has an area that
is double the area of his first snow fort. What could the
length and width of Duane's second snow fort be?

_____

4. **Write Math** ▸ How did you find the length of Kelly's dog run
in Exercise 1?

_____

_____

_____

Name _____

Area of a Dream Bedroom

Draw a diagram of your dream bedroom.
Include in the drawing a sleeping area, a closet, a bathroom,
and a study area. Label each area.

One square unit is equal to 1 square foot.

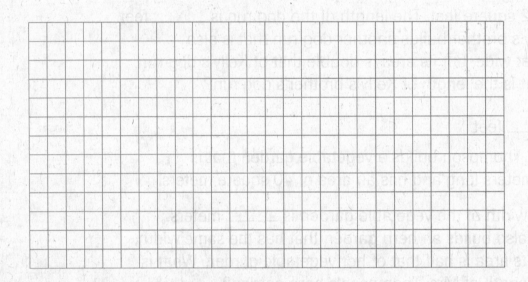

Use your drawing to solve the problems.

1. What is the total area of the sleeping
   area and the study area?

2. What is the total area of the closet
   and the bathroom?

3. What is the total area of the
   bedroom, except for the bathroom?

4. What is the total area of the bedroom
   you drew on the grid?

5. **Write Math** ▶ How did you find the answer to Exercise 4?

_____

_____

_____

Area and Perimeter Match-Up

Read the description. Write the letter of any shape that matches the description. More than one shape may match a description.

Description	Shapes

1. a rectangle with a perimeter of 16 units

_____

2. a four-sided shape with an area of 4 square units

_____

3. a four-sided shape with an area of 12 square units

_____

4. a four-sided shape with a perimeter of 8 units

_____

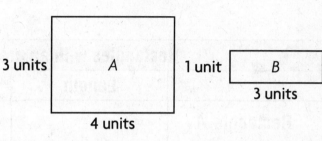
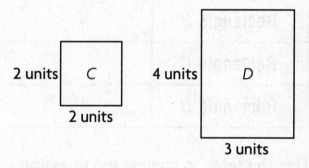
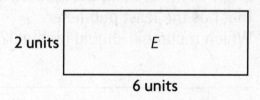

5. Stretch Your Thinking A four-sided shape is made from 24 unit squares. Using whole numbers, what is the smallest possible perimeter? Using whole numbers, what are the side lengths of the rectangle with the smallest perimeter?

_____

_____

Name _____

Area and Perimeter Comparisons

Find the length and width of 4 different rectangles such
that each rectangle has an area of 24 square units. Write the
length and width of each rectangle in the table. Then find
the perimeter of each rectangle and record it in the table.

Rectangles with an area of 24 square units			
	Length	**Width**	**Perimeter**
Rectangle A			
Rectangle B			
Rectangle C			
Rectangle D			

Use the table to answer the question.

1. Brian wants to build the rectangle
that has the least perimeter.
Which rectangle should he build?

   _____

2. Luke has 25 units of fencing.
Which is the largest rectangle for
which he can use the fencing?

   _____

3. Can Li build a square with an
area of 24 square units, such that
the side lengths are whole units?
Explain.

   _____

   _____

   _____

4. Ginger has 50 units of yarn.
She wants to use all of the yarn
as a border for one or more
rectangles. Which rectangle(s)
can Ginger build?

   _____

   _____

   _____

Shape Up!

Read the description. Then draw the shape. If the shape cannot be drawn, write the word *impossible*.

1. a ray with two endpoints

2. a closed shape with 6 line segments

3. a part of a line with two endpoints

4. an open triangle

5. an open shape with 7 line segments

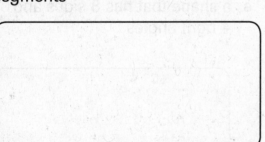

6. a closed shape with 3 line segments and a curved path

7. **Write Math** Nick says we cannot see any true lines in the real world. He thinks everything we call a *line* is really a line segment. Do you agree or disagree? **Explain.**

_____

_____

Name _____

Look at My Angle!

Read the description. Then draw the closed shape. If the shape cannot be drawn, write *impossible*.

1. a shape that has 6 sides and 3 right angles

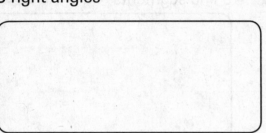

2. a triangle with 2 right angles

3. a shape that has 4 sides and 3 angles less than a right angle

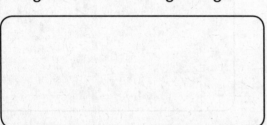

4. a shape that has 4 sides and 2 angles greater than a right angle

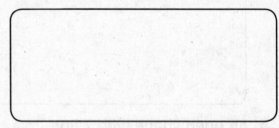

5. a shape that has 4 sides, 3 right angles, and 1 angle less than a right angle

6. a shape that has 8 sides and 4 right angles

7. **Write Math** ▶ Choose a shape from above that cannot be drawn.
Explain why the shape cannot be drawn.

_____

_____

_____

Name That Polygon

Sort and draw the shapes into two groups: shapes that are polygons and shapes that are not polygons.

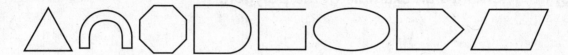

Polygons	Not Polygons

1. Name the polygons above.

——————————————

——————————————

——————————————

2. Draw a polygon that has six sides.

3. **Write Math** ▷ Can you draw a triangle that has 4 angles? **Explain.**

——————————————————————————

——————————————————————————

——————————————————————————

Side by Side

Decide if the polygon can have at least 1 pair of parallel sides, at least 1 pair of perpendicular sides, or both. Write *yes* or *no*. Then draw an example of the polygon.

1. triangle

parallel: _____

perpendicular: _____

2. quadrilateral

parallel: _____

perpendicular: _____

3. pentagon

parallel: _____

perpendicular: _____

4. hexagon

parallel: _____

perpendicular: _____

5. **Write Math** Choose another shape. Write your own exercise like 1–4 above. Then draw the shape to show the answer.

_____

_____

Quadrilateral Riddles

Read the riddles and name the shape that is being described.

1. I am a quadrilateral with exactly 1 pair of opposite sides that are parallel. What shape am I?

   _____

2. I am a quadrilateral with 4 sides that are of equal length and 4 right angles. What shape am I?

   _____

3. I am a quadrilateral with 2 pairs of opposite sides that are parallel, 2 pairs of sides that are of equal length, and 4 right angles. I am not a square. What shape am I?

   _____

4. I am a polygon with 4 sides and 4 angles. I do not have any pairs of opposite sides that are parallel. What shape am I?

   _____

5. **Write Math** ▶ Jerome drew a shape and described it as a square. Kayla described it as a rectangle. Luis described it as a rhombus. Can they all be correct? **Explain.**

   _____

   _____

   _____

   _____

   _____

   _____

Why Doesn't It Belong?

For each group of quadrilaterals, identify the shape(s) that do not belong and explain why.

1.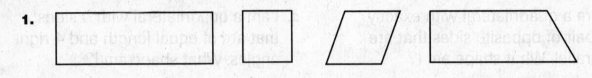

_____

_____

2.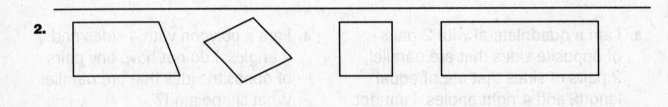

_____

_____

3.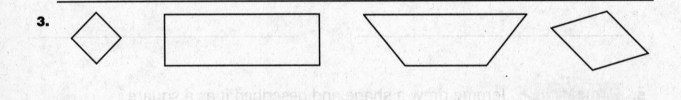

_____

_____

4.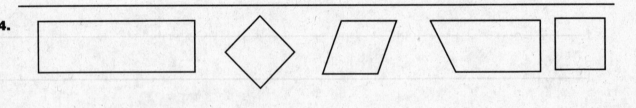

_____

_____

5. **Stretch Your Thinking** Draw your own group of four quadrilaterals. Challenge a classmate to identify the shape(s) that do not belong and explain why.

_____

Name _____

Sorting Triangles

Write the letter of the triangle in all buckets that correctly describe it. Each triangle can go in at least two buckets. Some triangles can go in more than two buckets.

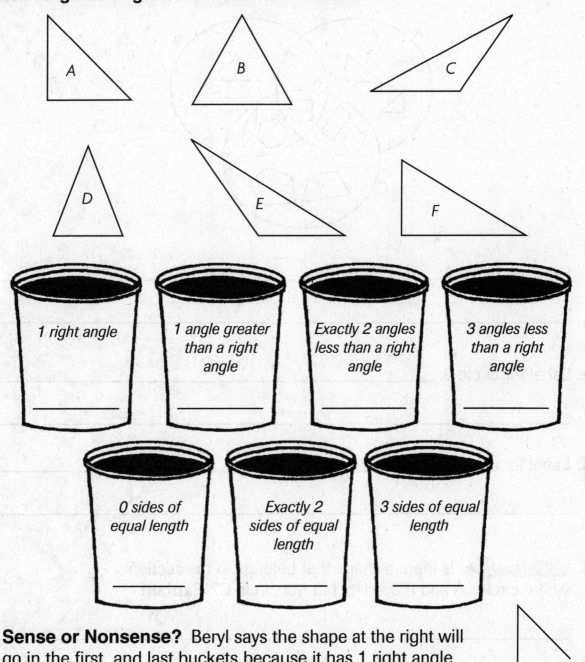

Sense or Nonsense? Beryl says the shape at the right will go in the first and last buckets because it has 1 right angle and 3 equal sides. Does her statement make sense? **Explain.**

_____

_____

E103

Triple Trouble

Some Venn diagrams have three overlapping circles. Look at the shapes in each circle of the Venn diagram below. Write a label for each circle.

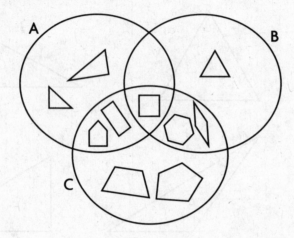

1. Label for circle A: _____

_____

2. Label for circle B: _____

_____

3. Label for circle C: _____

_____

4. **Write Math** ➤ Is there a shape that belongs in the section where circles A and B overlap, but not circle C? **Explain.**

_____

_____

_____

Name _____

Secret Message

Draw lines to divide the shape into the given number of parts of equal area. Write the fraction that names each part of the whole.

A 10 equal parts

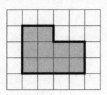

_____

F 4 equal parts

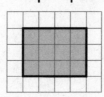

_____

H 8 equal parts

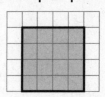

_____

I 6 equal parts

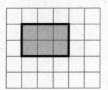

_____

M 12 equal parts

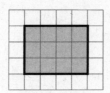

_____

N 2 equal parts

_____

S 5 equal parts

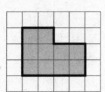

_____

T 9 equal parts

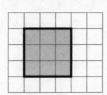

_____

U 3 equal parts

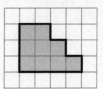

_____

**Write the fractions in order from least to greatest.
Use the letter for each fraction to write the secret message.**

$\dfrac{1}{12}$ ____ ____ ____   ____ ____   ____ ____ ____

 M ____ ____ ____   ____ ____   ____ ____ ____